Theme

HOUGHTON MIFFLIN
Reading
A Legacy of Literacy

Let's Count!

HOUGHTON MIFFLIN   BOSTON • MORRIS PLAINS, NJ

California • Colorado • Georgia • Illinois • New Jersey • Texas

Printed in the U.S.A.

ISBN: 0-618-07486-4

23456789-BS-06 05 04 03 02 01 00

Design, Art Management, and Page Production: Studio Goodwin Sturges

Contents

Nat, Pat, and Nan

by Elizabeth Kiley
illustrated by Fahimeh Amiri

Nat sat.

Pat ran.

Pat and Nat see Nan.

Nan! Nan!

Pat, Nat, and Nan sat.

Go, Cat!

by Elizabeth Kiley
illustrated by Nancy Speir

Go, Nan!

Nan ran, ran, ran.

Go, Pat!
Pat ran, ran, ran.

Go, Van!

Van ran, ran, ran.

Go, Cat!
Cat sat, sat, sat.

Pat and Nan

by Elizabeth Kiley
illustrated by Penny Carter

Pat sat.

Nan ran, ran, ran.

Nan sat.

Pat ran, ran, ran.

A fan!
A fan!

Go,  !

Word List

Story 1: *Nat, Pat, and Nan*

Decodable Words

New

<u>Words with -*an*:</u> *Nan, ran*

Previously Taught

Nat, Pat, sat

High-Frequency Words

New

and

Previously Taught

see

Word List

Story 2: *Go, Cat!*
Decodable Words
New
<u>Words with -an:</u> Nan, ran, Van

Previously Taught
cat, Pat, sat

High-Frequency Word
New
go

Word List

Story 3: *Pat and Nan*

Decodable Words

New

Consonant *f:* fan

Words with *-an:* fan, Nan, ran

Previously Taught

Pat, sat

High-Frequency Words

Previously Taught

a, and, go